Rhyme
& Reason

The Dream

Madhuri Fichtmuller

Dedication

For Jayan & Kai

Contents

Acknowledgements

Ajahn Brahm, Diana Cooper, Eckhart Tolle, Helen Schucman, James Redfield, Jeffrey Allen & Hisami, Jiddhu Krishnamurti, Jim Self, Kahlil Gibran, Kurt Tepperwein, Louise Hay, Michael Singer, Moritz Fichtmüller, Neale Donald Walsh, Nina Dul, Noah Elkrief, Osho, Parahamsa Yogananda, Paulo Coelho, Rick Archer & Guests, Sri Nisargadatta Maharaj, Swami Ramdev, Swami Sarvapriyananda, Swami Vivekananda, Thich Nhat Hanh, Tim Whild, Tony Parsons, Yongey Mingyur Rinpoche.

Thank you to my beautiful family and friends for this journey we share together.

Dream 3
Love & Oneness

Magnificent Days

On such magnificent days,
golden rays penetrate my thawing limbs.

The dizzying heights of summer,
it's easy to love all human beings.

My heart a vortex of soft humming,
in ecstasy from vibrations still strumming.
The sweet perfume, a hint of rose,
explosions of colour,
dazzling in amorous afterglow.

On such magnificent days,
it's easy to love myself.
Iridescent earth with shimmering beauty
reflects my image,
connects me to the wholeness within me.

As I wander indiscernibly through glistening fields,
the sunflower bows its sleepy head.
I bend to pluck a stem,
then in reverential stupor
return the bow with humility instead.

Animari – Come Alive!

This moment in time where every encounter
blows me off my feet.
A marvel!
A wonder!

A terrific world with countless souls.
A myriad of tales yet to be told.
In each individual, that beautiful spark,
glows to illumine the enchanted dark.

Soul mates galore,
admiration and awe.
Magnetic veneration,
this universal law.

Loving each soul without condition,
steeped in a oneness of unified vision.
In this vast tapestry of humanity,
Love, it becomes my guiding melody.

I hug all and sundry,
squeeze them so tight,
and cherish the sunshine,
the love and light.

This world feels miraculous,
exquisitely right.

The wow factor multiplies, growing in size,
harmony and abundance magnified.

Mind-blowing beauty, flora and fauna.
I catch my breath
as I dare to peep around the corner,
for the next miracle of grace
I can honour.

I consume the beauty,
devouring this sensory feast,
in a momentary fractal of time that has ceased.

Inexplicable phenomena,
Wondrous reality,
Torrential bliss,
Droplets of immortality.

A sudden realisation.
This Is Me!

Let the Party Begin!

I notice that dress
hanging up in the closet.
No recollection of buying it,
that I must confess.

Yet now that beautiful dress of my soul,
glistening in celestial light,
beckons.
A pull beyond my control.

Invisible to the touch.

I stretch it over my head,
erasing the filters of my mind
that expect too much.
Across my chest and arms,
and down to my feet.
It fits me perfectly.
Kindred souls finally meet.

It's on.
I'm safe.
I feel whole,
and I rejoice.

"Let the party begin!"

Music starts.
The lights they shimmer,
with this elixir of life,
regrets grow dimmer.

Surrender to the night,
rhythm takes hold.
Energy ignites
a sight to behold.

A celebration of life, in glorious light,
the night unfolds with pure delight.
Tonight, we're united in every way,
one body that moves and gently sways.

Dancing to the eternal beat of the heart,
I sense we've never been apart.
Sweet soul music,
ecstatic singing.
Intoxicated with bliss,
I dream
it's love I'm bringing.

Awareness

Sometimes I look around me
observing everything I desire to see,
when what it is I'm choosing,
is simply the specialness in me.

A mere idea of fragmentation,
keeping me attached to the temptation,
of seeing the apparition of bones and flesh,
purely dust and sand finely intermeshed,
and taking this to be you.

I could look beyond instead,
and see this is not true.

I have given you everything that you are,
simply by choosing thoughts
based on my experience thus far.

I recognise you when I look without the barrier
of my mind, that acts as some kind of separator.
Your essence divine, call it life itself,
inside this short-lived form, temporarily manifest.

So today I make a decision,
to see without thoughts or voices.
It's apparent, there seems to be only one of two choices.

Whether to conditioning I abide,
or whether consciousness guides,
I relax,
and let the present moment decide.

Relationships

You're so wrong, I'm totally right.
Nobody is right, let's fight.
You're totally right, I'm so wrong.
Nobody is wrong, opinions strong.

Who are these greedy generals in my head,
presenting scenarios, grossly overfed?
Tugging at my attention, this way and that,
relishing in conflict, mortal combat.

In a fleeting moment of stillness,
I sense it was only imposters I witnessed.
Generals pretending they knew,
when, in fact, they didn't have a clue.

Instructing me to march around,
restricting me to the confines of my mind,
instead of allowing me to break free
and realise that
which is truly me.

F*** this! ... I laugh and honour this moment,
in a space of compassion and razor-sharp discernment.
In the silence I wonder who it could be,
that's aware of these voices, muttering in me.

Neither me knowing you, nor you knowing me,
rather two mirrors reflecting each other,
in the vastness of this one, unpredictable sea.

I recognise myself in you.
I see your essence, which is mine too,
and I can love you,
unconditionally,
and myself, too.

.
.
.
.
.

For I am myself,
there's only one,
here,
as me
and you.

My School is Nature

I'm watching that Sequoia, how mighty she stands,
tall and proud, simple pleasures so grand.
As the currents of wind caress the trees,
the stream, she reveals how to flow with ease.

I'm watching the squirrel
quantum leap through the branches.
Never so happy as when taking chances.

I'm watching the rose amazed at what I see,
not a shadow of doubt she will blossom shortly.
Finding her solace in the nature of peace,
a sanctuary of possibilities, she navigates with ease.

I'm watching the horses,
oblivious to their pedigree,
and when I observe diligently,
I become aware of a certain stillness that's me.

I'm watching those robins build their nest,
meticulous teamwork,
a oneness that's blessed.

I'm watching the leaf spiral to the floor,
on the breath of the current,
there's no wanting for more.
Growth and decay, a beautiful dance,
like Sufi whirling,
left to circumstance and chance.

I notice the bramble,
in abundance she lives.
Overflowing with generosity,
she does nothing but give.

I'm watching that lily float over there,
elegantly bobbing, not a single care.
Exquisite beauty,
once rooted in sludge.
Rising high above that
which for most wouldn't budge.

I'm watching the dog, come wagging her tail,
full of compassion, only love prevails.

I'm watching the poppy sway in the breeze,
in total acceptance of who she is.

I'm watching the sky, the clouds passing by
and sensing the vastness, the deeper 'I'.

In this sacred school I feel my place.
One with Mother Earth,
in harmonious embrace.

That Sunday Morning

That Sunday morning washing our cars,
listening to Springsteen strumming his guitar.

Turn up the music to vacuum the seats,
warm sun on my shoulders, I soak in the heat.

Rays like fingers, massaging my back,
waves of serenity, assumedly laid-back.

You wipe the windscreen and scrape out the muck,
from biscuit crumbs and sweets,
in their wrappers still stuck.

I remember it clearly,
I remember that day.
We cleaned our cars silently,
few words we did say.

A strange moment with you, so connected I felt,
like our boundaries had merged
and were beginning to melt.

One with you,
such effortless grace,
in this silent, infinite, sacred space.

Then from the two that had merged into one,
a diminishing, apparent perception of none.

No me, no you, just nothing it's true.
No anything at all,
time adieu.

Vibrations at a frequency difficult to describe,
exultation and rapture, ecstatic inside.

Like an orgasm of the whole body,
with no body at all.
Explosion so great,
the whole universe so small.

Couldn't tell you how long 'til I was finally back,
with a hard, reluctant thud on the sticky tarmac.

Thursday Evenings

Simply an instrument,
the empty shell.
Life passes through me,
my song it tells.

We meet every Thursday
with the regular choir,
and sing individually,
somewhat discretely.

The piano divulges secrets with every key.
Confined emotions,
slowly set free.
The violin weeps her dulcet sounds.
Unrequited love,
once again found.

Sounds carry us into realms unknown,
each soul speaking a language of their own.

The conductor guides us into unity.
A higher order fills the spaces.
This melody
of individual stories,
transformed into a symphony
of divine voices.

Blessings

Thanks for this moment, gifted everyday.
Thanks for the birds gleefully chirping away.

Thanks for the earth, the flowers and trees,
sanctifying us wholly,
scents wafting on the breeze.

Thanks for the water, wind, sun and moon.
Mornings of idle bliss,
undulating into lazy afternoons.

Thanks for the music and laughter and dance.
The beauty of not knowing
that leaves everything to chance.

Thanks for the people who have graced my life.
Thanks for well-being, this body and this life.

Thanks for every single marvelous thing,
and that I can see myself in each miraculous being.

Thanks that I can share these wonderful gifts:
my love, gratitude, paradigm shifts.

Thanks that I have found a blissful freedom.
Thanks actually, for no apparent reason.

Exceptionally blessed with that which I care for.
Thanks that there's no part of me craving for more.

Dream 1
People & Society

This Ole Heart O' Mine

Adain, and Suggs to name but a few,
Alex and Blaine please join the queue.

Thanks to you all, for those wonderful days,
for breaking my heart in such spectacular ways.

And Deshal and Eli and Adaye and Jo,
well, I broke your heart and didn't even know.

My heartfelt apologies, for my total stupidity.
Was it a case of reverse serendipity?

I never intended to cause you distress.
Love's path, as you know, can be such a mess.

My heart was quite simply an open book,
and you were the ones to take a look.

The naivety of youth, with a love so free,
a love that was nothing more than raw energy.

The adverse endings some cut like a knife,
will never undo the best times of my life.

Those tears I cried, the weeping and whys.
Wouldn't be who I am today, without those goodbyes.

None of this could have happened without my small heart,
pumping away, dear wisdom she did impart.

Even as I wept, she continued to beat.
Wound still seeping, she watched over in my sleep.

Wound turned to scar, didn't let me conceal.
She carried on pumping 'til it eventually healed.

I thank you dear heart, for all that I am.
For exposing my vulnerability, without ever a slam.

For the love I've received and all that I've not.
You've taught me to love graciously,
and never to stop.

The Sage

I'm going around in a total spin,
thoughts reeling freely like a Dervish within.

What can I do about the poor grades in maths?
Antagonistic neighbours, downright sociopaths.

How can I possibly organise that meal for my friends?
Another five hours at work, I really should spend.

What about that constant headache of mine?
Will there be a day when I wake up feeling fine?

And the kids every minute on their latest smartphones,
whilst I watch in disdain, yet helplessly condone.

Not to mention my marriage, well we're lucky if we talk.
Should we stay together for the kids,
or should I just pack my bags and walk?

I can't find a solution, not a single answer,
to manage the chaos in my head,
this constant banter.

The guy at the bus stop I was venting to the other day,
sitting next to me, teeth rotting away.

He looked insane, couldn't properly speak,
and every pore of his body, of insobriety it did reek.

He listened quite politely, then asked …
"IF I MAY?"
Then at the top of his voice, he yelled,
"JUST GET OUT OF THE BLOODY WAY!"

Then he shouted again,

"STEP TO THE SIDE!"
"BOG OFF! SCRAM! SHOO!"

something else clearly implied.

I don't know what he meant, couldn't see no bus.
I wasn't obstructing him, so why the fuss?

'Om Sweet 'Om (ha-ha)

Wake up at sunrise or even at four.
Salute the sun, cobra, camel and more.

Tie my legs around my head in a rubbery knot,
followed by ginger tea, still piping hot.

Lentils on the menu for lunch every day.
Plastered smile, to hide the dismay.

I'm spiritual enlightened and earthed they say,
I stand in the garden and dig every day.

And when the energy ain't flowing right,
I know it's my chakras that must be too tight.

Epitome of goodness, I do the right stuff,
chanting my mantras, that's good enough.

Beneath the surface, beyond the façade,
there's a handful of yogis who play this charade.

I can twist myself up in positions you see,
and chant and sing,
and boast my sobriety.

Look inside yourself, that's what I preach,
if its eternal joy you want to reach.

I've looked inside.
Never seen further than the moss
growing between my teeth.
It's there when I floss.

With all that admiration, my ego swells.
A self-professed Guru,
no one can tell.

Dhotis, bindis, kaftans the rest,
Namaste, Namaste only the best.

Turbans, trinkets, all in white,
I'm up there in Nirvana with Curt Kobain all right,
yet not quite feeling all that delight.

Claiming to be perfect and ever so wise,
a spiritual pride that cannot be disguised.

With all due respect, there are those who are true,
who embrace this sacred art with integrity, too.
A hilarious journey,
realisation of self,
unity consciousness.

If only this I knew.

Smart Phone Samadhi

Dispirited, bored, feeling dismal inside,
I'll switch on the telly, my time I'll bide.
I see a smart-phone advert, smiling faces, wide-eyed.
That's got to be the solution to my boredom verified.

I button up my coat, and go out to explore
the treats that are waiting at the nearest smart-phone store.
Tablets and phones, pods and pads.
It's endless what's available, the stream of newest fads.

No concept of gadgets, I hover vulnerably,
until an ambitious sales-assistant convinces me
to buy the latest, spectacular, something G.

Boy, am I thrilled,
unable to keep my pride abreast,
It's elated my status to
'up there with the best'.
Holding it nonchalantly for everyone to see,
I'm cool, I'm worth it, flying high, exultantly.
Lost in the glow of this digital haze,
I succumb to connection in this virtual space.

This elation and gratitude remains for all of two weeks.
Though I'm clutching it tightly,
like sand through my fingers,
it idly leaks.

To add to it, I've discovered there's a whole lot more.
They're waiting in queues
outside that famous store.

For apparently, it's out, the latest version,
G+1 it's called, with added scintillation.

The irresistible allure, that's got to be the cure.
This facile device is bunk, my acquisition premature.

I'll join the queue again, this time precisely informed,
and buy the latest version,
my boredom once again transformed.

And so the story goes on, they've come and they've gone.
Nothing permanent,
yet an improvement on the previous one.

I've climbed the whole ladder,
reached top rungs with the new GS.
Though how long this will last,
is simply anyone's guess.

The length of its sojourn simply depends
upon when boredom and misery once again descend.
This unquenchable yearning for material, for more,
proves ephemeral gadgets are not the cure.

For peace of mind and lasting happiness,
I'll have to look somewhere else
...at least that's my guess.

Bring on the Drama!

An apparent illusion, maybe surreal.
The pictures you see, the colours you feel.

So, choose your story, have fun with it.
Success, fame and fortune,
the sky's the limit.

Let drama play out and the story delight
with its twists and turns, under a shimmering moonlight.

Heroes and villains, an audience enthralled,
suspense and intrigue, 'til the final curtain call.

It doesn't change the essence, it doesn't matter,
all roles required for this three-dimensional chatter.

It's up to you to choose the way.
You're the one performing out there on the day.

If in your script, you are hated and left out,
you'll create a story that leaves no room for doubt.

Yes, everyone does hate you, you'll see that it fits.
Yet, they would love you too,
simply change the words of your script.

You're feeling despondent, choosing to see it that way.
In this present life, it's only you with the say.

With vibrancy and joy,
create your intention
and feel your wholeness,
with simple attention.

Saint or Sinner,
Pauper or Queen,
It makes no difference,
simply choose your dream.

Listen to your script, does it suit you today?
Is it in harmony with that for which you pray?

Re-write it jubilantly, you're the Director of the play,
directing its debut, out there on Broadway!

No Less, No More

That's me, here I am, dark eyes standing small.
Here I take my place on the wheel of this world.

Glimpsing the shooting star whiz through the sky,
I recognise myself and don't ask why.

Observe my surroundings, I take it all in.
From the depth of my soul, I comprehend my origin,
acknowledging the misrelation to the colour of my skin.

But people still ask, they always do,
Where are you from?
I can't seem to place you.

Unvocalised thoughts, derisory stares.
You don't belong here. To say it, they won't dare.

Not quintessentially English, your skin is too dark.
A colony perhaps of the British Monarch?

I stand there bewildered.
I am English, can't you see?
A true Petriburgian.
And yes, there is Indian and African in me.

But who cares anyway, what difference does it make?
Is there a need for categorisation of my heritage,
for God's sake?

Why bother with "buts," why do I even need to justify
my existence,
amongst people who only care to classify?

I'm everything actually, the whole world is me.
The sum of all continents to put it aptly.

And where I'm from, is where my heart feels connected.
Where I feel safe, at home and not separated.

A citizen of this world, that's me to the core.
A human being on planet Earth.

No less,
No more.

If you don't Enjoy it, What are you Doing it For?

That tiresome job, I know I'm only there
to make ends meet.
Would rather be elsewhere.

Party tonight, room crammed to the rafters.
Small talk at the bar, discussing disasters.

Get-togethers that end in a rut,
'cause nobody can actually stand each other's guts.

Glancing at watches, counting down the time.
Gosh we must be going, it's the kids' bedtime!

Fear of upset, what will people say.
Hard to tell the truth without offending in some way.

Seemingly uncaring it could be construed,
through long-standing conditioning, deeply imbued.

In pursuit of our goals and lofty ideals,
chasing impish dreams, forgetting what's real.

I've made a little promise that's only for me.
It's to not waste time being where I don't want to be
and to love myself always, unconditionally.

To never forsake me or put myself last,
or doormat myself so others can feel large.

I refuse to throw myself under the bus,
or listen to that voice, the critical judge.

I love you I do, there's no other truth.
It's just that I love myself equally, too.

And, if I can't do what I truly enjoy,
I will simply make sure I enjoy what I do.

That Which I'm Not

I'm not perfect…Neither are you.
Never claimed to be…How about you?

You're disappointed I see…had another view of me.
Foolish, trivial…to be taken advantage of easily.

You'd like me to be quiet, not say a word.
Smile, look pretty, seen and not heard.

I've shattered the illusion, "how could I possibly be,"
that which I am, authentic and free?

Of flesh and blood, no deity, nor priest.
Never claimed to be…anything but me.

True to myself, impulsive and hot,
loving and kind,
though sometimes I'm not.
Open your eyes and you will surely see,
just how hundred percent I can be me.

Neither good nor bad,
I simply am.
At the end of the day
it's all I can.

So, hate me,
I'd prefer that when choosing my lot,
to someone who loves me,
for that which I'm not.

Thank God

Have I ever seen you God?
Many times I've tried.
Up there on your throne,
high above the sky.

Created the world in merely six days,
one helluva bein' you have to say.

Are you even alive, or long gone dead?
Ever thought of applying for another job instead?

And what do you look like?
I've often wondered.
Black, white, brown, maybe blue?
Even this I've pondered.

Sitting up there, having a laugh I guess,
watching us pawns in this crazy game of chess.

And what is your job, I mean what do you do all day,
apart from stand at the gates and shoo people away?

Like palace guards, sounds quite boring to me.
Certainly not my cup of tea.

Amazed by you, I'm a bit confused as well,
cause you've created a wonderful world
that's as miserable as hell.

Did something go wrong
or was it always meant to be this way?
For there's some huge contradictions going on,
dare I say.

If I were responsible for all that shrapnel,
wouldn't I right now be sitting in hell?

Do you see us all,
one more f****d up than the next?
Fighting and greed,
don't care about the rest.

Do you see the pandemics, catastrophes and troops
and onlookers on their phones,
trying to capture the scoops?

And the fear, the madmen, the utterly depressed
and the rest with their looks,
simply totally obsessed.

Do you see us all sitting there, stuffing our faces with chips,
watching on telly some crap, or binge-watching Netflix?

And then praying to you when things go wrong.
It's up to you to fix it our whole life long.

It can't possibly be true, there can't possibly be a you
that's so powerful,
yet chooses suffering anew.

At least not a you, that's as unforgiving as me,
with no idea of love and self-responsibility.

That's why I'm guessing that you were created by me.
In fact, it's actually quite plain to see.

You created us and we created you,
to make this world function as we'd like it to do.

This world is simply a creation of our minds,
with little to do with the creation of mankind.

Heavenly power, nourishing Earth as your child,
you've given us the freedom to develop our own mind.

As a tiny infant, we've taken those first steps.
Into a child we've grown, with challenges beset.

Now a troubled teen with a mind of our own,
Rebellion,
Frustration,
Innocence outgrown.

And as we pass through this phase as well,
and mature into adulthood and reasoning impelled,
you'll still be there to guide us through,
as veils are lifted,
and dawn breaks anew.

The Mirror

Never met anyone like you before,
and probably never again.
A beautiful heart brimming with love,
topped with an illumined brain.

I SEE YOU
A reflection so wonderfully clear.
A soul worthy of love,
with nothing to fear.

Your energy glows, reaching out far,
igniting a wonderful spirit.
I adore your laughter, creativity, and joy,
not to mention your pencil-sharp wit.

Across your chest, that beautiful scar,
a reminder of who you truly are.
Each imperfection, a wondrous story to tell,
a testament to life thus far.

Your eyes enigmatic, don't hide how you feel,
the door to your soul,
all truths revealed.
Insatiable beauty, I'm under the spell.
Your very being, it rejuvenates my cells.

You dance with grace,
every limb of your body,
as if nothing matters,
so effortlessly.
No longer bound by worldly expectations.
Love, it is your true liberation.

Your skin, your face, your hair as it sways.
I LOVE YOU
every minute of every single day.
You're out of this world and stunning you know.
Yet, I don't remember ever telling you so.

So, I'm telling you this as you look back at me.
Please, open your eyes and finally see.

The Best Interest of the Kids

How could you, you floozy, you hustler, you cheat?
Met someone else, have you?
Are they keeping you sweet?

Wasn't I good enough?
What did they have that I lack?
More time, sweet words, a bulging six-pack?

A foolish mistake, is that what you say?
Too late for regrets, you won't get away.

I'll make you suffer, if it's the last thing I do.
Take you to the cleaners, get my revenge on you.

Nobody dares do something like that to me.
You'll regret this big-time, just wait and see.

You won't see a penny, I'm broke don't you know?
Forget about maintenance, that's the end of outflow.

Changed the locks on the doors, don't you ever come back.
Clothes and toys for the kids,
Oops,
must have forgotten to pack.

Your belongings still here, it's plain to see,
that they always,
quite simply,
have belonged to me.

Kids need new shoes, huh?
well get them yourself.
McDonalds are recruiting,
get your resume off the shelf.

I'm getting a lawyer and bleeding you dry.
Custody of the kids, don't even bother to try.

Play Station I'll buy them, and tablets and treats.
I'll explain to them quite clearly
that you are the cheat.

Then I'll get them in court
where they can tell the judge out straight,
that they'd rather live with me,
than with you and your mate.

It's damn worth the thousands I'll spend on legal fees,
to make sure in this lifetime
you never get custody.

Mediation a joke,
nothing left to discuss.
See another side of me now,
never knew me so callous.

They're stuttering and twitching,
biting skin round their nails.
I'll continue fighting,
let madness prevail.

The nights they can't sleep, are upset and cry,
then I'll tell them who's to blame.
There's only one bad guy.

And if anyone should dare question the things that I did.
Well,
I was only ever acting
in the best interest of our kids!

An Incident

Part 1 - The Alternative

Incidents happen, that's life you know.
From my heart, I apologise, I didn't mean it so.

I'm aware that I hurt you, please know it wasn't intended.
Is there anything I can do?
Please let me know how I can mend it.

You're one with me,
we're both the same.
With every single hurt I cause,
it's me, too,
that feels the pain.

Thanks for the apology, nothing to forgive my friend.
We're all human, it happens,
your humility I commend.

Whatever we do, we're not our behaviour.
We couldn't have acted differently,
our friendship does not waver.

All is well,
I still love you, my friend.
No need to worry, everything on the mend.

I thank you,
and love you too.
You're dear to me.
This foolish moment has left no debris.

Part 2 - As So Often Happens

Same incident happens, that's life you know.
No need for communication, my reputation on show.

I'll hate you instead, never speak to you again.
Foolish actions, unforgivable, punishment required.
Amen.

Retreat into corners, I'll not come out anymore.
Could get complicated, scared my imperfection may show.

Convince the world how appalling you are,
no talking, nor smiling, all contact is barred.

Trepidation they're laughing and looking at me.
I'll never get close to anyone again, my promise you'll see.

Turmoil within, I feel so much anger.
Like mud on my feet, it entrenches me further.

I've incarcerated myself, my mind is not free,
and what I don't realise is that
I'm the jailor with the key.

Fear and hate, inner pain that I feel.
Read above for an alternative,
'cause only love is real.

Never Upset for the Reason you Think[*]

Never upset for the reason you think.
Ponder over these words, next time you kick up a stink.

It's driving me insane, they're out there again,
pesky kids playing football, triggering my migraine.

Highlighting my misery, I'd better go out.
Shaking my fists, I'll have a good shout.

Hurtling abusive words, I've filled them with terror,
I can see it in their faces and now I feel better.

Late in the evening, curtains drawn tight,
I'll sit with my husband in silence all night.

Our marriage is certainly not going well.
To tell you the truth, we're going through hell.

But I can't get out, I'm worthless you see.
In the meantime,
my thoughts are getting the better of me.

Something happened last week, I'll explain it briefly.
We had a small row, and once again he abused me.

The police I called, they were here in a flash.
For the first time I talked, and explained the whole clash.

The restraining order he got
should keep him at arm's length.
I've kicked him out of my life,
found my freedom and strength.

This marriage, old beliefs, all of it I quit,
as I finally realise,
yes, … I am worth it!
I thought myself in and thought myself out.
Meaningless thoughts, I could probably do without

As for the kids playing outside, doesn't bother me at all.
Oh, they've kicked it over again,
let me go fetch your ball!

*A Course in Miracles

Marriage

The ultimate golden cage, some say without a doubt.
Those outside wanting to get in,
those inside frantic to get out.
A love bound by rings,
fervent expectations these bring.

Hollywood romances, fairytale endings,
we'd all like to believe.
We'll ride into the sunset,
and happily ever after we'll live.

Self-delusion I believe.
By this, I mean
seems perfect on the outside,
when, in fact, faulty at the seams.

Starting with the vows, we promise to love our whole life.
Got to admit it's not easy, could get us into strife.

Out of sheer honesty I mean,
not because our feelings aren't strong.
No-one knows what love is,
so, we could have it completely wrong.

Are we confusing it with attachment,
or maybe even domination?
Believing we can complete the other,
a common misconception.

So, we're promising something we don't quite understand,
like promising a gem we may never hold in our hands.

And we're promising something for the rest of eternity,
even though into the future we cannot see.

At best, we can say, we feel strongly today,
and that we sincerely hope it stays this way.

S.O.S.

**Restore your harmony and inner peace,
nothing to do, past is released.**

**Live in the moment, nothing to fear,
accept who you are, it's okay to shed a tear.**

What a load of shit, you don't have a clue.
Don't you have anything better to do?

Get a freaking real job just like me,
with power, and influence, and responsibility.

A hard day's work …24/7,
don't see the kids … home at eleven.

Earning good dough, work for the CEO.
Irreplaceable in fact, until I get sacked.

But that'll never happen, it's plain to see.
There's no way on this planet,
they'll survive without me.

Lost all my hair, blood pressure high,
burned-out and proud, palpitations nigh.

I'm lining their pockets, wads bulging so fat,
whilst you waste your time on some meditation mat.

You don't fit in, averse to the strife
of despondent people…hypocrisy rife.

A wretched life, I'm happy with it.
Can't stand those around me, nor spiritual shit.

Have a disagreement, I want to hold on.
You've already let go and are moving on.

I can't stand you at all, you uncivilized lot.
Searching for truth, when I'm fundamentally not.

Cup half-full, love & light,
bloody disgrace … you're not quite right.

Complaining and griping, need a bigger car.
Must upgrade the house,
that's who we are!

Floor needs replacing, only stop to think,
back submissively aching, marriage on the brink.

Flash on the outside, inside I'm poor,
with my constant, insatiable craving for more.

I don't need you highlighting everything I'm not.
That's why I hate you and your crazy lot.

Yet in the depths of despair when I'm all alone,
you'd better come quick,
and save my soul!

Helicopter

Hovering out there, watching our kids.
There's ice out there, danger!
Watch out you might skid!

Some call us curlers, clearing the ice.
Smoothing the way, removing all that ain't nice.

My child needs to have all that I didn't,
I'll solve all their problems before they've arisen.

Enough stimulation and a Harvard CV,
must lay the foundations before the tender age of three.

All wishes granted before they've even left the lips,
there's no way my child will endure any hardship.

Yet suffering and ache, difficulty and strife,
just like happiness and joy,
an intrinsic part of life.

Welcome the problems, don't clear them away.
Trust your child to face them every single day.

They're tougher than you know, and independent, too.
With your love and support, they will get through.

And maybe make mistakes some of the days
whilst finding their truth along the way.

So instead of hovering, show them what you know.

Stand back, have faith, trust and let go.

Don't Shoot the Messenger

When whatever I do
is never enough.
When whatever I say
offends in some way.

When walking through the door is enough to trigger you,
to awaken the festering pain anew.

You can be hurt by nothing but your thoughts.
Ghost nets in your mind, tangled up in knots.

Stop shooting those arrows, they cut through the heart.
Each time a little deeper, pulling us apart.

Only you can get yourself out of this rut.
Don't shoot the messenger
or slam this door shut.

Take a moment to simply reflect.
I'm merely a conduit,
please spare me reject.

Dream 2
Thoughts & Emotions

Anger

What is that thing that brews up inside
and then lashes out after generations denied?

Disguised as depression, sadness and frustration,
feelings of powerlessness, with no liberation.

Could it be centuries of pain unreleased?
Growling, hungry,
waiting to be unleashed.

Barbed roots so thick, fiercely tangled inside.
Chains that bind,
a spirit confined.

From lifetimes back I feel it has come.
Oppression, repression, denial of freedom.

What can be done to release that force?
Pent up emotions, years of remorse.

Screaming, tapping, punching a pillow,
exercise, journal, help shift that sorrow.

That will make sure the root does not grow.
To pull it out may need more though.

Complete identification is like wood to the fire.
Reduce those flames, let awareness get higher.

Step aside, observe, embrace and see,
the anger is not you, you are separate and free.

Follow it within, to its original source,
to transform this suffering into its guiding voice.

Old patterns lose force, flow away like water.
Over time, there'll be less to pass on to your daughter.

Love 2.0

Is it a well that I can fall in?
Can it be shared or is that a sin?

Can I love you and everyone else?
Or are you exclusive,
a trophy on my shelf?

"I belong to you" they say and "you belong to me."
Two kids, the family unit,
we're as happy as can be!

Our love reserved for us, no reason to share.
In this world of "not enough,"
"why … there's nothing left to spare!"

Makes no sense, I think you'll agree.
Love is, quite simply,
Divine energy.

The force of life,
the reason we're here.
A dance of the soul,
so preciously clear.

Enough to go round, that's easy to see.
The fifth element,
nothing left of me.

Joyfully living, instead of existing.
Abundantly shining, instead of resisting.

Love gives you wings and sets you free,
takes you higher, allows you to be.

A state of being, I'd prefer to think,
as I put away my cups and wipe down the sink.

What's the (F***ing) Point?

What's the time? … It's already four!
I guess I should get out of bed.
Can't face a shower, I'd rather do nothing,
and avoid the day ahead.

Pitiable fridge, completely empty, not even a pint of milk.
Dry cornflakes will do, it's good enough.
Just please,
don't ask me to think.

I try so hard, day and night,
yet deep inside nothing feels right.
I question my purpose, I question my worth.
What is the point of this life on Earth?

A hub of madness
where worlds collide.
Am I just here,
along for the ride?

Don't want to talk, nor my brain to holler.
I switch off my phone
and veg here alone,
in my den of squalor.

The truth is,
I really don't care.
I sit, and at the blank wall
I stare.

I convince myself about tomorrow,
when I'll have the motivation maybe,
to do the things I can't face today,
and start over again properly.

In these darkest moments,
I beg to find
a reason to keep going,
a purpose that is mine.

Nothing is for real, that's plain to see.
Simply no reason to get out of bed for me.
So, help me, please,
set me free.
Just help me,
to step out of this nightmare called me.

The numbness
of this day,
will it last forever?
What's the f***ing point
when there seems no hope of change,
not ever?

Confused, unsure, blinded by the world,
…there's gotta be more than this!
Time has seized a part of me,
and my eyes can longer see what they miss.

I search for a depth, a relationship that's true,
and hope for a way to follow through.
My walls they're up, can't let nothing in,
yet, somehow still longing for that connection within.

I search for the point in each droplet of time.
Choices I make feel like lessons divine.
Is anguish my teacher that helps me evolve,
until inner peace becomes my resolve?

Some say, *tomorrow's another day,*
and that when I wake up, I'll see.
Yet, no matter how wide I open my eyes,
this doesn't seem to apply to me.

'Cause if I manage to get up again,
feeling exactly the same way,
I'll ask myself what day it is
and it will,
still,
most definitely,
be today.

Tomorrow never comes, and as I'm almost there,
it moves, quite simply,
further away.

Thoughts

Nothing in your words can hurt me,
nor the tone in which you speak.
Nothing in your actions can hurt me,
nor avoidance, ignorance, or any other technique.

Nothing in this world can hurt me,
neither fear, propaganda, nor dynamic shifts.
There's nothing here, external to me
that can impact my bliss,
an intrinsic gift.

I have come to realise a truth,
the simple key.
It's merely my thoughts
that cause injury.

I could simply let go
and watch them float by,
like capricious clouds,
in a sullen, autumn sky.

One thing is true.
My peace depends on it,
on each inherent thought,
and my choice whether to engage with it.

Fear

Fear,
this fear,
making me quiver.

Leaves outside, voraciously shaking.
I'm under my duvet, physically quaking.

Dark still of the night, engulfed in my fright
of what might be,
too painful to see.

Ghosts of my imagination,
filling me with dread,
whispering with glee
to drowsy thoughts in my head.

What should I do?
Scared to death I confess.
Well, shake, be fearful, let it take over, I guess.

What else is there to do?
I suppose nothing at all.
Just be here, pay attention, until the end of nightfall.

And watch 'til it passes, like a tree in a storm.
Notice the energy that has duly transformed.

Observe this fear and know it's not real.
A swindler, totally impotent, only energy they steal.

With a dark cloak and dagger, surrounding your space.
Away from deep love and light they doth chase.

Shine that spotlight in their face and embrace them,
that fear.
Like a coward in the night,
they'll stealthily disappear.

Bring on That Smile, Don't Forget to Laugh!

There's a wonderful thing that happens
every time someone smiles.
It's contagious, builds a bridge that goes on for miles.

A feeling of joy, I delight in its presence.
Feels wonderful inside, connects to my essence.

Look on the bright side, don't forget to laugh,
relish in that smile, on everyone's behalf.

Let's say for example, you've damaged your knee.
Well, you could choose to see it as a grand opportunity.

Feet up for the first time, well and truly deserved.
Monarch of the castle, let yourself be served.

And let's say, unfortunately you've lost your job.
You're furious, go on have that little sob.

Then when you're done with feeling glum,
bring on that smile and let in the sun.

For you may have just finally found the time,
to do those things you've dreamt of your whole lifetime.

Spend time with the kids, maybe even write that book.
Those burning desires, they're still there if you look.

So what if your partner has shamefully dumped you.
Look on the bright side, no more compromising to do.

Stop being so flippant, who's going to pay the bills?
I'll never get another job, worry firmly instilled.

There's no way on this planet
I'll find the man of my dreams.

My clock is ticking,
my body falling apart at the seams.

Too many hopes, too often failed.
Too many dreams, that never prevailed.

Well, let's take a look and think about it logically.
The probability of a positive outcome
is nothing less than 50/50.

And since nobody has a magic ball
that can tell the future once and for all,
it's pretty clear that it makes no sense
to focus purely on potential problems immense.

Body sensations, they flicker like dots,
hopping around on a particular spot.

Thoughts that connect them often beguile,
choosing the frown instead of the smile.

Excitement into Fear,
Joy into Worry,
Bliss to Anger,
Mind in a flurry.

So, wouldn't you rather focus on light,
than fill yourself up with fear and fright?

One day it won't matter if there's sunshine or rain,
or whether the rose has thorns or petals again.

You'll realise that you are
both day and night.

There is no such thing
as darkness without light.

Lonely

I woke up this morning in a funny kind of space.
Weird, empty, feeling out of place.

I started to wonder, for I'm definitely not alone.
What could be going on?
I pondered on my own.

Is there anyone out there who feels what I feel?
Who has the inkling that nothing's for real?

Is there anyone out there who sees what I see?
The madness prevailing,
or is it just me?

How can anyone who has a brain in their head,
not notice most people are walking around dead?

Corpses at work, tap, tap on the keys,
climbing the ladder, hey boss, take a look at me!

Believing the tabloids, drip-feeding their brains,
inciting false hatred for financial gains.

Corpses on Insta', checking for friends,
fear of missing out, going round the bend.

Corpses in Starbucks, another espresso, please!
Pouting in the mirror, I'll take a selfie.

Personality polished until its glistening.
The perfect sum total of all past conditioning.

Corpses in suburbs, 2.1 kids,
working all hours to earn extra quids.

Corpses in playgrounds, *"my kid is way ahead!"*
"Mine too, he's so sweet,"
clobbering his mate around the head.

Discussing the teachers, rumours and natter,
CVs mapped out for kids for whom nothing matters.

Must get the best job, and have all I do not.
Money and success, fame the whole lot.

Corpses out shopping
tottering on Louboutin's,
head to toe in designer gear,
sporting asymmetric grins.

Corpses on bikes, sweaty and smelly.
Corpses in gyms, watching the telly.

What seems to matter are money and looks,
caught up in their dramas, right there on the hook.

Boasting and shaming, ungrateful and sad.
It's black or it's white, must be good or it's bad.

I guess the one thing fundamentally different about me,
is that I can't give a shit.
I'll explain more, you'll see.

I can't give a shit as hard as I try,
that there's a new designer store opening up nearby.

I can't give a shit as hard as I try,
that the royals are scratching out each other's eyes,
since that notable interview that caused an outcry.

I can't give a shit as hard as I try,
that some celeb spent a fortune
on her wedding to that guy,
or sent boy racers to space,
without the blink of an eye.

Is there anyone out there who feels deep inside,
that there's got to be more than ego and pride?

What about this planet, compassion and love,
understanding the bigger picture within and above?

I can't be all that different
as it appears to be.
We're all part of the same ocean,
there's nothing special about me.

So, if you, too, have forgotten
and are feeling kind of low,
I'm always there, a part of you.
Simply this,
I hope you know.

Harmony

Waving the white flag,
I call an end to the war within this town.
Differing groups upon whom I gladly frown.

I call an end to the war raging within these four walls,
between loved ones, zealous, unrelenting brawls.

The single problem of separation.
The single solution of unity.
I recognise this,
and every crisis is solved immediately.

I relinquish useless guns and armour,
that chain my mind to fear,
and lay them down gently
at truth's frontier.

I break down the stone walls I have built
to keep me safe.
I no longer need saviour and protection,
or to defend my faith.

On a journey of harmony in the present moment,
I embark.
As conflict and resolution unite,
I end the war,
blazing
within my own heart.

Truth

She is right,
and so is he.
Yet they have opposing views.
Who should I believe, what should I do?

The tree in the woods cradles my perplexed thoughts.
In the foliage of her compassionate arms,
I no longer feel distraught.

As she whispers softly through the hanging willows,
"the brilliant mind does not always know."

I contemplate this in stillness of the moment,
whilst basking in the satisfaction
of a life so transient.

And as the wind weaves its way
through her emerald leaves,
I sense the wisdom of her heart
as she gently breathes.

Teardrops

Tears fall as I realise I am enough,
even though the taste of inadequacy remains on my lips.

Tears fall as I apprehend my inner queen,
even though they call me the pauper.

Tears fall as I recognise my beauty,
even though the societal mirror reflects a strikingly different
image.

Tears fall as I comprehend my wisdom,
even though they say intelligence belongs only to the select
few.

Tears fall as I value my potential,
even though inherent structures crush my hopes and dreams.

Tears fall as I hear my voice for the first time,
above the hum of a society
that sings to a completely different tune.

Tears fall as I feel the veil of ignorance separating us,
waywardly sanctioning truths it has not experienced.

Tears fall as I realise it's not my fault,
and even more as I realise,
I alone,
cannot dry this salt.

Forgiveness

I forgive you both, that's my personal choice.
"Don't let them off the hook!"
says a small little voice.

It's not about that,
I don't see it so.

It's purely a decision on my part to let go,
of the pain in my heart,
and the disappointment caused.
The beauty of friendship momentarily paused.

There's a hurting within, inner child some may say,
waiting for a sign that you regret your behaviour that day.

A nice person, I thought, behaving momentarily dumb,
or maybe the other way around?
Difficult to fathom.

Harsh feelings have been given permission to depart,
together with the realisation, we're actually worlds apart.

My rucksack feels lighter,
my eyes somewhat brighter.

And if there's one thing, I've learned from this,
It's the lesson of self-compassion I shouldn't dismiss.

"Be gentle on yourself sweet child," they say.
"You'll probably look back and smile one day."

Nothing to forgive in the big scheme of things.
Consciousness experiencing life as a mere human being,
acting purely out of past conditioning.

Dream 4
Lucidity

Free your Mind (and the Rest will Follow)

Take a pen in your hand
and give yourself ten minutes' time,
to write down the thoughts in your head,
so sublime.

Hundreds of cogs whirring at the same time.
An insight into humanity at its absolute prime.

Have a read of them,
you'll find things so amazingly mad.
Wouldn't dare to show your best friend
the scribbles on your pad.

Scared of that place where we can't feel the light,
being stuck in the dark, fills us with fright.

Film or museum, gym or a club.
Any entertainment will do, meet you at ten down the pub.

I need to feel alive, from these thoughts I must flee.
More to distract me now than ever in history.

Great boldness required to face my own nudity.
No restrictions to the unpleasant feelings inside of me.

Fear of being unlikeable, unworthy or blamed.
The fear of not enough, or simply insane.

I could observe my mind,
watch my thoughts that don't stop.
I might see my attachment eventually drop.

Thinking is Overrated

Either you know something
or you don't.
The wisdom of many lifetimes,
with the sparkle of a newborn child.

Dewdrop pearls glisten inside.

Thank You My Angels

Thank you my angels, for pointing the way.
For not holding on to a thing that I say.

For your unconditional love, that I feel in extremes.
For your belief in abundance, and for living your dreams.

No expectations you hold, simply born of creation.
Full of joy and hope, and not yet frustration.

Courage to sing, dance and play,
you feel your emotions in every way.
Live in the moment,
here today.

Your honesty and trust in all that you see,
your belief in the best never ceases to humble me.

Don't take things personally, no expectations you hold,
able to let go, be free and be bold.

Open hearts and jokes, don't take yourselves too seriously.
No inhibitions,
not yet afraid to show your vulnerability.

Nothing to forgive, you love for the sake of it.
Hardship and pain, big deal you don't make of it.

Small things in life bring you so much joy,
pure enthusiasm, energy and hugs ahoy.

Don't beat around the bush, say it as it is, I agree.
True to yourself, the greatest honesty.

Wouldn't it be great if we learned a thing or two,
by watching you angels
and taking the cue.

We could learn to fall in love with life again,
instead of suffering and apparent pain.

A lesson from our children every single day,
would peel away layers that have turned into clay.
Fear and self-loathing, and not being enough,
judgement, incessant thinking,
dense, material stuff.

We owe it to ourselves to be blissful and free.
We were once kids.
Can't be that difficult, you agree?

Take a leaf from their book, instead of reproach.
Let us be the pupils, instead of the coach.

God bless you, my angels, for showing me the way.
For reminding me who I am,
I thank you,
each and every day.

And for giving me the wonderful gift that I see,
when I look into your eyes,
and glimpse eternity.

Joy

Sitting in my favourite café,
reminiscing over poignant moments
that have slipped away.
Shrinking and worrying about what may come my way.

When an innocent child knocks at the door,
of a tired heart that apparently feels no more.
Hey, she grins,
do you wanna play?

I know,
I've been away far too long,
and in the meantime,
so much has gone.

But guess what?
I refuse to visit you secretly,
and what's more,
I demand that you stay with me.

Let's hold hands and never let go.
In this symphony of life, our joy will grow.

Let's stay up until sunrise, as temperatures begin to warm,
and cherry blossom bursts into morning song.
Let's listen to the chorus of divine blackbirds,
merrily chirping along.

Let's watch the flowers bathe in the morning dew,
unleashing love in our hearts anew.

Let's chase our dreams, no matter which way,
and embrace this sparkling, magnificent day.

Let's walk barefoot through clear streams,
humming joyfully at the top of their voices,
as diamond droplets adorn our heels,
and the sun gleefully rejoices.

Let's stand at the edge of the cool sea
and gradually tiptoe in,
then immerse ourselves unashamedly
and let glorious renewal begin.

Eager lungs, they taste the chill,
as we squeal with delight and shiver within.

Let's look up at the moon
and the stars as they fall,
and sense light through the cracks
and feel the home call.

Upstream

Swimming upstream, struggling, gasping,
thrashing away for your life.
Let go, relax, surrender, start floating,
allow the end of strife.

> Don't worry in which direction you go,
> trust wherever it leads.
> Relinquish what might perceivably happen,
> even when going full speed.

Life will take care of every moment,
a guarantee that is truly assured.
Can't get lost down the river, you're part of it,
it's holding you safely, secured.

> Revel in the mysteries of life,
> it's happening just as it should.
> Nothing to do or try to control,
> life is intrinsically good.

A total faith in life unconditionally.
A total faith in others' divinity.

> Accepting *what is,* the delight of life,
> no longer a need to ask *why?*
> A captivating oneness with life itself,
> let go, spread those wings and soar high.

The Journey

I'm off the train, no longer the same,
have let go of some of what was in my brain.

Though not yet at the final station.
Which way now to the ultimate destination?

No belongings, no baggage, just a small backpack.
No possibility of ever turning back.

I'm standing here in the middle of nowhere.
Lost and alone, I confront my ultimate fear.

Trembling, I don't know which way to turn.
For simple directions, I desperately yearn.

A signpost ... I must be close, it's got to be.
Yet the signpost only has one arm,
pointing directly at me.

I recognise this place, full of peace, striking beauty.
Only last time there was something missing.

Unmistakably me.

Agape

Taking in the view, in the beauty of the light.
Gazing at you, I sense my delight.

Captivating sensations pervade my body,
until thoughts take charge
and implore that I have you.

At that precise second when thought shapes sensation,
I'm hooked with desire,
for this seraphic creation.

Leaning into the sensations, I do not deny
the beauty of the view, the form passing by.

Relishing the splendour of the sensory onslaught,
in the space that doesn't allow interference of thought.

Then I am free to love.

Agape.

Silence

Sit with me in silence, just sit there and feel.
If you're serious about knowing me, knowing me for real.

Don't mind there's no mind, logic gone astray.
Words riding on your thoughts, carry you further away.
Truth gets lost.
Confused translations have nothing to say.

Just absorb who I am, don't say a word.
Nothing but space, free like a bird.

Words are unnecessary,
a case of less is more.
Only stillness is required to access my inner core.

A faded portrait of the heavenly sky.
Sit with me,
in silence,
for the utmost, divine reply.

Two become One

Hate myself.
Love myself.
Know myself.
Be myself.
Be.

Nothing

Nothing to do,
you always knew.
It's clear.
Be here.
Don't interfere.

Dream 5
Totality & Nothingness

Equanimity

What am I to you,
with the things that I do?

Seraph, scoundrel, saviour, or cad?
Oh, how I make you ecstatic and mad!

I'll give you the choice what you want me to be.
I'll give you the choice what you decide to see.

Take your pick from the information gleaned.
Light of your life, maybe despicable fiend.

Which glasses you choose depends upon you,
for I remain static,
nothing else to do.

I really don't mind, I'm actually nothing you see.
Just an empty vessel,
reflecting you onto me.

Om Shanti Om

This production line,
some call it the mind,
churns out endless problems.
Self-created,
Unrelated.

Then looks for solutions
to address the illusion,
creating more confusion.

The dog chases its tail,
to no avail.

In the vastness beyond the mind
does activity cease.

...

There lies peace.

Timelessness

The ultimate smooth criminal, you'll never catch her.
Nimble, light footed, gone in a whisper.
Trace her, track her, anticipate future crimes planned.
She'll still slip through your fingers,
back home to Neverland.

Antagonize where she is, remember past crimes.
You won't find her, ever, experience sublime.
Elusive is her game, genius some would say.
From the temporal dimension actually,
so she'll always get away.

Not yet the master though, for she always leaves behind
a distinct piece of evidence of her masterminded crimes.
Transparent enough for everyone to see,
simple remnants of the human body.

Who am I?

Where are you my rose, my beautiful rose?
I planted that seed with intentions that you grow.

With plenty of fertilizer, water and earth,
light, minerals, preparing for birth.

Yet now when I look, there's no rose I see.
Just petals, a stem, three leaves, an ovary.

Where are you sweet rose?
Show me signs of your creation,
because I don't seem to see any actual manifestation.

Or are you already there, a continuation of life?
Well, who am I then, if I dissect with a knife?

Am I these bones, my skin, my flesh?
Maybe my brain,
or my thoughts manifest?

Cause when they fall away,
like leaves on a tree,
well, there's still a whole lot left,
a whole lot to me

Not so much an individual creation,
but of subtle parts,
a delicate manifestation.

With a certain nothingness pervading my cells.
A simple observer of me,
as nothing else.

The Tightrope

When falling off,

is enough

to get me back on.

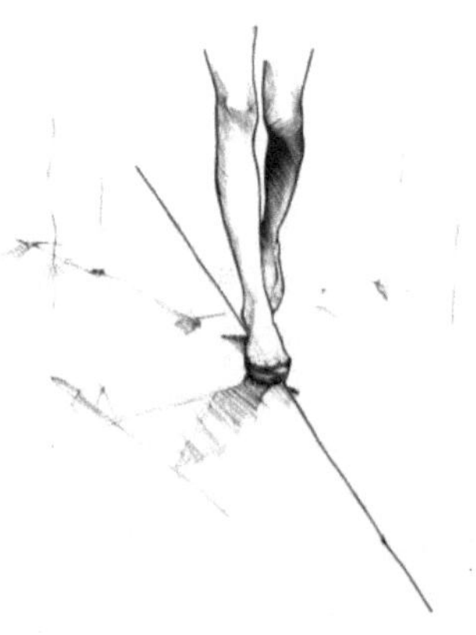

Mind the Gap

Watch this space!

That's Me

That's me, dreaming this dream.
That's me, projected onto the screen.

The wave that melts into the vastness of the sea.
The one that doesn't know, that's me.

Let the waves roll in and gently go.
Playing the game of life,
I remain so.

Existence itself, walking and talking,
in every single form,
consciousness illuminating.

The reflection out there, that's a part of me.
And also, the observer, the one who sees.
All that
and far beyond.
Infinite nothingness of pure eternity,
from which life is born repeatedly.

There are no gaps, duality, polarity,
just emptiness,
totality,
universally me.

Light of the light,
sun illuminating the moon at night.
Lighting up the mind,
my world shines bright.

Being, Consciousness of any degree.
Questions to all answers.

That is me.

Umbilical Cord

The umbilical cord is cut and clipped,
withdrawing consciousness from my thoughts.
They fall away,
leaving only that which is real.

I no longer move through time.
In stillness,
time moves through me,
ceases to offend.

Infinite

Never born,
I cannot die.
Time caves in,
encapsulating the Now.

Stillness.
Infinite peace.
Duality ceases,
in the Wholeness
of what is.

Liberation

Dear Christ, Dear Buddha,
God in whatever name so sweet.
I finally understand that You and I,
we will never meet.
Watching, waiting, reading and seeking,
a waste of time, this desire I was keeping.

For when I am there, you are not.
And when you happen, I will not.

6 Tabula Rasa

Doubt

No doubt.
Nothing to figure out.

Essence

When I sit, I sit.
That's all there is to it.

Freedom

Laughing like a clown,
in all the wrong places.

Deeper.

Deeper.

Tabula Rasa

Bliss

No Title

●

Wake up!